YOU ARE 7 AN HERO

EARN 12 HERO BADGES

INTERACTIVE

INSPIRING STORIES FOR 7 YEAR OLD BOYS

KYLIE CROSBY

Badger Kids
Big Stories for Little Badgers
badgerkids.com

For information about special discounts for bulk purchases, please contact Badger Kids via business@badgerkids.com

Title: You Are 7 and a Hero!
Interactive Inspiring Stories for 7 Year Old Boys
Subtitle: Motivating Short Stories With Badge Challenges
To Boost Confidence, Courage and Real-Life Skills
ISBN Identifiers: 978-9918-0-1387-6 (e-book) | 978-9918-0-1388-3 (paperback) | 978-9918-0-1389-0 (hardcover)

TABLE OF CONTENTS

A NOTE FOR GROWN-UPS

This book is written especially for seven-year-olds, using vocabulary tuned to a typical second-grade reading level.

It is child-safe, free from slang, and carries no hidden religious or political agenda.

The only focus is encouraging a boy's growth in everyday life.

Each story ends with its own **Hero Lesson** and a **Badge Challenge**.

These are small, real-world actions that let the boy practice important life skills like courage, kindness, and responsibility.

When he completes the steps, he earns a **Hero Badge**.

Your role as the grown-up is important:

- First, talk with him about the Hero Lesson and how it might apply in his own life.

- Next, help him plan how to do the Badge Challenge and make sure it is safe and appropriate.

- Finally, when he has completed the steps, give your approval to collect the Hero Badge.

This keeps the activities guided, supported, and meaningful.

You are warmly encouraged to join in.

Read together, talk about the Hero Lessons, and celebrate each Hero Badge he earns.

These interactive moments of encouragement are where the stories truly come alive.

If you and your boy enjoy this book, I would be grateful for a quick review.

Even a few words help other families discover it and let me know my work is making a difference.

I personally read every single review and look forward to reading yours!

With love,
Kylie Crosby

Now, let's help your boy grow into his best self.

WELCOME, 7-YEAR-OLD HERO!

Are you ready for an adventure?

This book is packed with exciting stories about 7-year-old heroes just like you!

You can read them on your own, or ask a grown-up to read with you.

Maybe you got this book as a gift... or maybe your friends showed you their amazing **Hero Badges**!

Every 7-year-old boy can be a hero.

That means you too!

But before you can collect these Hero Badges, you'll need to earn them!

Here's how it works:

- At the end of every story, you'll learn a **Hero Lesson**. Think about how it could be true for you, or talk about it with a grown-up.
- Next, follow the steps in the **Badge Challenge** to try it out in real life.
- When you're done, tell a grown-up what you did. If they approve, the **Hero Badge** is yours!

Can you collect all 12 Hero Badges?

Each one is available in 3 cool versions:

- **Black-and-white coloring badges**:
    - These are already included in the book, you can color these Hero Badges however you like!
    - If you want a separate, larger page to color, you can check the print version. You can then hang them up and be proud of them!
- **Official full-color badges**:
    - Print the official Hero Badges in color and show them off! You can also hang them on the fridge, your bedroom wall, or anywhere else you are allowed.
- **3D printable badges**:
    - If a grown-up has access to a 3D printer, you can ask their help to 3D print your Hero Badges and hold them in your hands!

Choose the version you like best,
or collect them all!

Get your Hero Badges here:

Just scan the QR code or visit:

badgerkids.com/7hero

BADGER KIDS
BIG STORIES FOR LITTLE BADGERS

MATEO'S FIRST DAY AT A NEW SCHOOL

The school hallway buzzed like a beehive. Lockers slammed, sneakers squeaked, and kids shouted to their friends.

Mateo gripped his backpack straps tighter. Today was his first day at a new school, and he didn't know a single person.

Many other kids were already laughing with friends, sliding into seats together, whispering secrets.

Mateo slipped into the back row and stayed quiet all morning, hoping no one noticed him.

Whenever someone looked at him, his cheeks burned. He ducked his head and stared at the scuffed toes of his sneakers. *What if no one talks to me at all?* he wondered.

At lunchtime, Mateo carried his lunchbox outside and picked a lonely bench. Around him, kids raced across the playground, shrieking with laughter.

Mateo hunched over his lunchbox, wishing he could shrink as small as an ant.

Then he remembered what Mom said that morning when she dropped him off at school:

"Being brave doesn't mean you're not scared. You can be brave by trying — even when you feel scared."

Mateo lifted his head and spotted another boy by the swings. The boy's shoulders drooped, and he kicked at the dirt like he wanted to disappear.

Mateo's heart thumped. His legs felt heavy, but he pushed himself up and walked toward the boy.

"Hi," Mateo said, his voice wobbly but his smile steady.

The boy glanced up, surprised, then gave a shy smile. "Hello."

"I'm Mateo," he said quickly. Then, gathering courage: "Want to sit together?"

The boy nodded. "Okay. I'm Max."

They headed back to the bench and opened their lunchboxes. Max noticed Mateo's tacos and said, "Those look tasty. I had tacos last night!"

Mateo blinked in surprise, then smiled. He had worried the other kids might think his food was strange or tease him for it.

But Max didn't mind at all — in fact, he looked excited to see something familiar. For the first time that day, Mateo didn't feel so different.

Mateo snapped his cookie in half, crumbs spilling into his lap. He offered the bigger piece to Max, who looked like he discovered treasure.

"Thanks!" said Max, already munching on the cookie. Then, with a hopeful grin, he asked, "Want to play tag after?"

Mateo's smile spread so wide it made his cheeks hurt. "Yes!" he said, nodding fast.

After finishing their lunch, the two boys ran across the playground while laughing loudly.

Another classmate asked, “Can I play too?”

Mateo waved him in. “Of course! The more, the better!” he shouted over his shoulder.

By the end of lunch, Mateo wasn’t alone anymore. In class, Max slid into the seat beside him, and Mateo smiled, feeling like they were friends already.

They tackled math problems together, whispered answers during reading, and teamed up in gym class, cheering each other on.

When the final bell rang, they marched out the doors side by side, already talking about tomorrow.

Mateo thought back to Mom’s words and smiled. Today, being brave had given him something better than he had imagined — a new friend.

HERO LESSON

**Being brave means trying,
even when you feel scared.**

What about you?

- When did you feel shy or nervous at school or somewhere new?
- What helped you to try and be brave anyway?

BADGE CHALLENGE

Choose one brave action to
earn the **Brave Starter** Hero Badge:

O Be the first to say hi to someone in your class, especially if they are new.

O If a classmate looks lonely, invite them to sit with you or join your game.

O Share something small with a friend at school (like a snack, a toy, or a funny story).

HERO BADGE

This badge is only yours when you've completed one of the brave actions.

What did you do to earn this Hero Badge?

____

____

Ask a grown-up to approve below and start coloring!

You earned the Brave Starter badge!

Signed by: ____________________ Date: __________

SAM LEARNS THE CALM PLAN

Sam sat in a circle with three other kids in Miss Lee's office. She was the school counselor. She was kind, and today she was sharing ways to stay calm.

On the windowsill were pots of small plants. Their green leaves looked fresh in the sunlight. On the shelf were a few books and a jar of glittery sand that sparkled in the sun.

Miss Lee smiled. "Sometimes your face feels hot, your chest feels tight, or you just want to shout. That's when it helps to have a calm plan."

Sam pushed up his glasses and leaned forward. He wanted to know more.

"**Step one**," Miss Lee said, "is to name your feeling. For example, you might say, 'I feel mad,' or 'I feel nervous.' When you name it, it starts to shrink."

"Name it?" Sam asked. "Like saying it out loud?"

Miss Lee nodded. "Exactly."

Sam wasn't sure saying a feeling could really work. He gave it a try and whispered "mad" quietly. It felt a little lighter, like putting down a heavy backpack.

"**Step two**," Miss Lee said, holding up a balloon. "Pretend you have a balloon like this in your chest.

- "Breathe in slowly, and imagine the balloon filling with air.
- "Hold your breath, like holding a full balloon for a moment.
- "Breathe out slowly, and let the balloon shrink until it's empty.
- "Hold your breath again for a moment, like holding an empty balloon.

"In, hold, out, hold. That's one balloon breath. You can do it again and again until your body feels calmer."

The kids copied her, puffing their cheeks and pretending to have balloons in their chests. Sam felt his chest grow and shrink as he breathed slowly and steadily.

"**Step three**," Miss Lee continued, "is to do one small thing next. For example, if you're mad at a friend, you might decide to walk away and cool down.

"If you're worried about a hard question, you might raise your hand and just ask for help. One small thing can make the big feeling smaller."

Later that week, Sam's soccer ball bounced high, then landed in the neighbor's garden. He couldn't reach his ball, and now he couldn't play anymore.

That made his face feel hot and his stomach feel tight. He almost wanted to kick the fence. But then Sam remembered what Miss Lee had told him about using the calm plan when his body felt this way.

"Step one: I feel frustrated," he said quietly.

For step two, he imagined a balloon in his chest and breathed:

In — the balloon filled with air. Hold — he held the full balloon. Out — the balloon shrank smaller. Hold — he held the empty balloon.

He took two balloon breaths until his shoulders relaxed.

Then he whispered, “Step three: one small thing.” Sam walked to the fence and called politely, “Excuse me! Could you please pass my ball back?”

The neighbor smiled, tossed it over, and Sam grinned.

At dinner, Mom noticed. “You look calmer, Sam.”

He nodded. “I used my calm plan. Name it. Balloon breath. One thing.”

Mom squeezed his hand. “That’s a steady heart.”

Sam smiled and pushed up his glasses. His body might feel hot or tight again tomorrow. But now he had a plan — and it worked.

HERO LESSON

You can find a way to feel calm when strong feelings show up in your body.

What about you?

- When did you last feel upset?
- What happened and how did that make you feel?

BADGE CHALLENGE

Next time you're upset, try all three steps of the calm plan to earn the **Steady Heart** Hero Badge:

O Step 1: Name your feeling out loud.

O Step 2: Take one or more balloon breaths: Breathe in... Hold... Breathe out... Hold...

O Step 3: Do one small thing to help yourself feel better.

HERO BADGE

You will only unlock this badge when big feelings show up and you remember to try the calm plan.

What did you do to earn this Hero Badge?

____

____

Ask a grown-up to approve below and start coloring!

You earned the Steady Heart badge!

Signed by: ____________________ Date: __________

CALEB'S SMALL ACT OF COURAGE

The lunchroom was loud with clattering trays and noisy chatter. The smell of spaghetti filled the air while kids hurried to find seats.

Caleb slid into a spot at the end of the table. He was about to bite into his sandwich when he noticed a boy standing nearby with his tray.

The boy's name was Daniel. He had a stutter, and sometimes it took him a while to get his words out.

"C-can I sit here?" Daniel asked.

Before Caleb could answer, another kid grinned and called out, "Oh, look everyone, it's D-D-D-Daniel!"

A couple of others snickered, laughing into their hands. Daniel's face turned red, and he stared down at his tray.

The mean words stung. Caleb's cheeks turned hot, and his body went stiff. Caleb knew that was what bullies did — they made someone feel small.

Caleb wanted to stay quiet and look at his sandwich. But he saw how Daniel's shoulders slumped and how his tray shook in his hands.

Caleb's stomach twisted while his heart thumped in his chest. He wanted to shrink into his seat, but something inside pushed him to move.

His legs felt heavy, but he scooted over. "You can sit here," he said, looking at Daniel instead of looking at the kids who had laughed.

Daniel's eyes lifted. "Th-thanks," he whispered, and slid into the seat next to Caleb.

The snickering stopped when Caleb gave no attention to it. Soon the table was filled with the ordinary sound of chewing and chatter again.

Caleb let out a breath. It hadn't been a big speech. Just a few words. But Daniel was smiling now, and that made Caleb feel lighter inside.

Later that afternoon, Caleb saw Daniel standing near the fence, kicking at the dirt. A group of kids were starting a basketball game, but no one had asked him to join.

Caleb jogged over, heart beating fast again. "Want to play?" he asked.

Daniel hesitated. "I'm not g-great at basketball."

Caleb grinned. "Neither am I. We'll be buddies on the same team."

They ran onto the court together and joined in. Caleb passed the ball to Daniel but he fumbled and dropped it.

Daniel looked disappointed as the ball went from player to player. Then Caleb caught it and tossed it to Daniel again.

This time, Daniel managed to catch the ball and quickly pass it to another teammate, who scored with a clean swish.

Their team cheered, and another boy clapped Daniel on the back for the good pass.

By the end of the game, Daniel had a wide grin on his face. Caleb felt proud of his buddy.

Caleb didn't do much that day — he just said a few words and showed a bit of courage. But it had made a big difference to Daniel.

HERO LESSON

When you show even a small act of courage, you can help someone feel stronger and less alone.

What about you?

- Have you ever seen someone being teased?
- What could you do to help without giving the bully more attention?

BADGE CHALLENGE

Do one small act of courage to earn the **Buddy Courage** Hero Badge:

O If someone is teased, don't join in. Invite them to sit or play with you instead.

O When teams are being picked, invite someone who hasn't been chosen yet.

O Say something nice or offer help to someone who seems nervous.

HERO BADGE

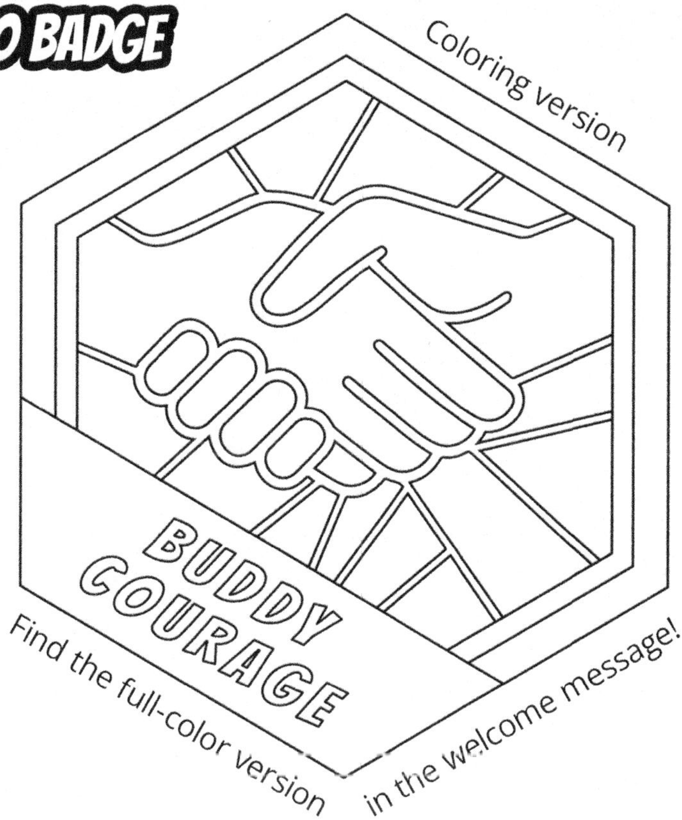

This badge is yours when you've completed one of the small acts of courage.

What did you do to earn this Hero Badge?

____

____

Ask a grown-up to approve below and start coloring!

You earned the Buddy Courage badge!

Signed by: ____________________ Date: __________

NOAH FIXES A FRIENDSHIP

After school, Noah went into the bedroom and tossed his backpack onto his bed.

His step-brother Jordan sat on the rug, with pieces of a broken spaceship scattered around him.

“You stepped on it!” Jordan snapped, holding up the smashed pieces.

Noah frowned. “I didn’t!” he said. Then he remembered. He had stepped on it that morning, when rushing to leave for school.

It was an accident, but he knew it was still his fault. His head went cold, and a shaky feeling spread in his chest.

"You don't care about my stuff," Jordan muttered, trying to fit the pieces back together.

Since their parents got married last spring, sharing a room hasn't been easy. Sometimes it feels like they are more enemies than brothers.

Noah wanted to say it was Jordan's own fault for leaving it on the floor.

Then Noah remembered what happened at Dad's apartment last weekend.

They were about to play catch outside when Noah spilled juice across Dad's papers.

"Sorry!" he said quickly, without pausing. He hoped Dad would forgive him easily so they could hurry out the door.

Dad stopped him with a hand on his shoulder. "When you make a mistake, you need to own it, Noah.

"Just saying 'sorry' fast doesn't fix much. You didn't even look at me."

Noah squirmed. They only had two days together.

Noah just wanted to go outside and play with Dad.

Dad went on, "Want to know something that helps me when I make a mistake? I try three steps."

"You still make mistakes too?" asked Noah.

Dad answered, "Of course I do. Everyone makes mistakes now and then. Here's what I do:

- "**First**, I say what I'm sorry for.
- "**Second**, I say why it mattered.
- "**Third**, I say what I'll do next time.

"It shows the other person I mean it. You can give it a try sometime."

Dad's words came back to Noah as he looked at Jordan's hunched shoulders.

He sat on the edge of the bed, his voice quieter. "Okay. I did step on it. I'm sorry for breaking your ship."

Jordan froze.

"It mattered because you worked really hard on it,"

Noah added, his throat tight.

"Next time I'll watch where I'm going."

Jordan blinked. The anger in his eyes faded as he asked, "You... you really mean that?"

Noah nodded. "Yeah. Want me to help rebuild it?"

Jordan's shoulders eased. After a pause, he pushed the pile of blocks between them. "Okay. But you have to find the missing wing."

Click by click, the ship began to take shape again. Noah and Jordan were leaning in close, working side by side. The new ship turned out bigger and stronger than the old one.

Later that night, Mom peeked into the room to check on them. Both boys were laughing on the floor while flying the new spaceship over their heads.

Noah felt lighter. Dad was right — saying sorry the right way fixed more than a ship. It helped rebuild his friendship with Jordan.

HERO LESSON

Saying sorry the right way can help fix a friendship.

What about you?

- When did you last argue with a friend or family member?
- What helped you make up afterward?

BADGE CHALLENGE

Try the three-step apology to earn the **Trust Fixer** Hero Badge:

O Step 1: Say, "I'm sorry for..." and admit to your mistake.

O Step 2: Say, "It mattered because..." and explain why it hurt or upset the other person.

O Step 3: Say, "Next time I will..." and promise a better action.

HERO BADGE

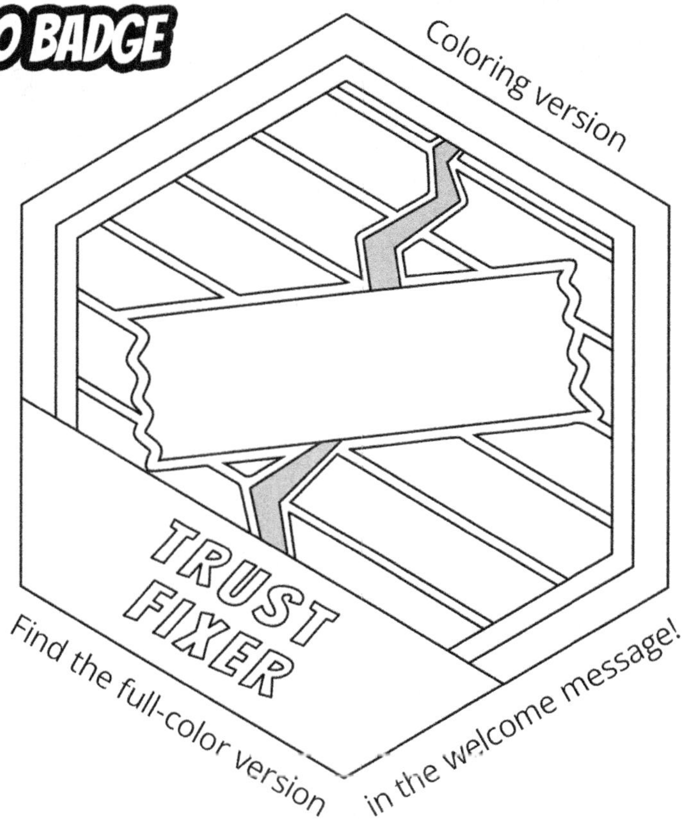

This badge is only yours when you try the three-step apology for real.

What did you do to earn this Hero Badge?

____

____

Ask a grown-up to approve below and start coloring!

You earned the Trust Fixer badge!

Signed by: ____________________ Date: __________

OWEN'S BOOK OF DRAGONS

Owen sat at the kitchen table with a notepad open in front of him, ready to draw a dragon. He gripped his pencil so tight it squeaked on the paper.

He sketched the wings, but one came out bigger than the other. He rubbed hard with his eraser, leaving gray crumbs on the page, and tried again.

This time the dragon's tail was too short. Frustrated, Owen let his pencil roll off the table and slumped in his chair. "I'll never get it right," he muttered.

Dad peeked over from the sink. "Looks like a good start," he said.

"It's not!" Owen sighed. "It doesn't look like the

dragon in my head."

Dad wiped his hands and sat beside him. "You know, big things don't show up all at once. They grow from little steps." He pointed out the window.

Owen leaned back in his chair. In the corner of the backyard stood the small tree they had planted last spring. Its thin branches now had more green leaves than before.

"It's taller now, isn't it?" Dad said. "Each day it grows a little more. Drawings grow the same way — one step at a time."

Owen picked up his pencil again. He drew just one claw. It looked okay. Then he added the second. Slowly, his dragon began to take shape...

The next afternoon, Owen sat on the steps of the back porch. The wooden steps felt warm under his legs and the sun on his back made him relax.

He had his notepad on his knees to give it another try. The wings were still tricky, but they looked a little better than yesterday's.

At the same time, his little sister Ruby was walking around the yard. Her shoes brushed through the grass while she hummed the tune from her school program.

She sang the first line clearly, but when she reached the high note her voice squeaked and broke.

She scrunched up her face and stomped her foot. "I'll never get it right," Ruby said.

Owen looked up from his drawing. "That's what I said about my dragon!"

He flipped the notepad around and held it up to her so she could see yesterday's dragon next to today's.

"See? They're not perfect, but each one is a little better."

Ruby's eyes brightened. "So my song can grow like your dragons?"

"That's right," Owen said with a grin.

By the end of the week, Owen could turn the pages of his notepad and see dragon after dragon.

Some leaned sideways like they might fall over. One had a long and funny nose. Another had ears that stuck out like giant spoons. A few looked almost the way he wanted.

Ruby's song still had a few pauses, but now she could sing from the first word to the last without stopping.

Owen smiled at his dragons, and Ruby smiled at her almost-perfect song.

They were still practicing, but they could see they were growing, one step at a time.

HERO LESSON

Practice makes progress —
step by step.

What about you?

- What's something you'd like to get better at if you keep practicing?

BADGE CHALLENGE

Do all three steps to
earn the **Patient Builder** Hero Badge:

O Step 1: Choose one small thing you want to build, draw, or practice.

O Step 2: Work on it a little bit every day for seven days.

O Step 3: At the end, show your progress to a grown-up or a friend.

HERO BADGE

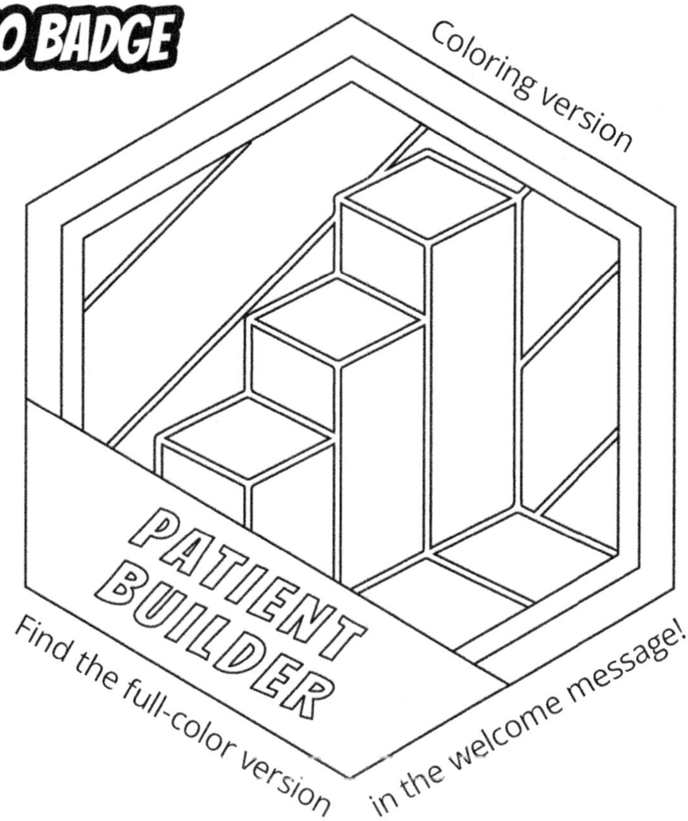

This badge is yours when you finish all three steps on the previous page.

What did you do to earn this Hero Badge?

____

____

Ask a grown-up to approve below and start coloring!

You earned the Patient Builder badge!

Signed by: ____________________ Date: __________

MARCUS BUILDS HIS STRENGTH

The whistle blew, shrill and sharp, and the kids burst across the playground. The relay batons flashed from hand to hand.

The baton smacked into Marcus's hand, smooth and cold. He gripped it tight and took off.

He ran hard, but his belly jiggled, and his chest felt tight before he got halfway. His sneakers thumped the ground as he stumbled to the handoff, gasping for air.

"Nice try, Marcus," Coach said kindly. But Marcus could see the other kids cheering each other as they finished. He stared at his sneakers so they wouldn't see his face.

That evening, Marcus dropped onto the couch and reached for his game controller.

Dad poked his head in. “Tough gym class today?”

Marcus shrugged. “I’m just no good at running.”

Dad sat beside him. “You know, you didn’t get good at your video game in one try either. You practiced.”

He nodded toward the door. “Want to try ten minutes outside before dinner? Just to the park and back.”

Marcus groaned. “I’ll be tired.”

Dad smiled. “That’s the point. You’ll get stronger every time.

“You can’t build a strong body in one day. Just like Grandma’s Sunday roast, it takes time and care. Bodies come in all shapes. Yours can be strong too.”

“Okay,” Marcus muttered, “but only to the bench.”

Dad laughed. “Deal.”

They jogged together to the corner of the park. By the time they reached the bench, Marcus's chest burned, but he was smiling anyway.

"There you go! That wasn't so bad," Dad said.

The next day they ran to the park again. Marcus's legs burned, but he made it further than before.

On the third day, Dad was busy. "Sorry, champ, I can't come tonight."

Marcus thought about playing a video game instead. But he wanted to keep going, so he grabbed his sneakers and said, "That's okay. I'll ask Andre."

Andre, his neighbor across the hall, grinned when Marcus knocked. "Sure! Let's race to the park."

Just then, Andre's mom tied her running shoes. "Perfect timing, boys. I'm heading out for my run. You two can jog with me."

Dad waved from the doorway. "Have fun, champ. Stick with Andre's mom and be careful."

They set off together. Andre's braids bounced as he laughed, and Marcus pushed himself to keep up.

At the park bench, Andre's mom smiled. "I'll go for a few laps around the park. You stay here where I can see you." She waved and set off at an easy pace.

Marcus watched her go, his eyes wide. He bent over, hands on his knees, catching his breath. "Doesn't your mom get tired?" he asked between breaths.

Andre grinned. "She runs almost every day. She says it makes her feel strong."

Marcus kept staring after her, still breathing hard. He thought, *If she can run lap after lap, maybe one day it will feel that easy for me too.*

At the next gym class relay, Marcus made it to the handoff without slowing down, and his chest didn't ache as much. He felt proud of himself.

Coach slapped him on the back. "Great effort today, Marcus. Keep it up."

Marcus smiled wide. He wasn't the fastest. But he knew he was making progress.

Just like in his video game, he was leveling up with every run.

HERO LESSON

Exercise makes every body healthier and stronger — one step, one lap, one practice at a time.

What about you?

- What's one small way you could move your body more this week?

BADGE CHALLENGE

Move your body for 10 minutes a day, for 3 days in a row to earn the **Strong Runner** Hero Badge:

O Day 1: Walk, jog, or play outside for 10 minutes.

O Day 2: Move again for another 10 minutes.

O Day 3: Do it one more time for 10 minutes.

Tip: Ask a parent or friend to join you to make it more fun!

HERO BADGE

This badge is yours when you move your body for 3 days in a row.

What did you do to earn this Hero Badge?

____

____

Ask a grown-up to approve below and start coloring!

You earned the Strong Runner badge!

Signed by: ____________________ Date: __________

ALEX AND THE WIGGLY NUMBERS

Alex tapped his pencil against the desk, staring at the worksheet. The first problem read: 23 + 8 = ...

But for Alex, the numbers seemed to wiggle and dance when he tried to read them.

All around him, kids were already bending over their papers. Their pencils scratched fast across the pages.

Some kids didn't even pause, and seemed to fly through the worksheet. But Alex still hadn't written a single answer.

Even though he had practiced, the numbers still jumbled together. His chest tightened, and a hot lump formed in his throat.

Mrs. Carter walked past and smiled gently. “Keep trying, Alex. Remember, you can use your blocks if you need.”

He didn’t want to. Some kids didn’t need blocks. He didn’t want to look slow. But leaving the page blank would feel worse.

He stacked two groups of ten, then added three, then counted out eight more. “Thirty-one,” he whispered and wrote it down.

Not quick. But correct.

Later on the playground, his friend Jamal shouted, “Race you to the swings!”

Alex shook his head. “I’m too slow. At math. At reading. At everything.”

“So what?” Jamal said with excitement. “You’re faster than anyone on the monkey bars. Remember yesterday? You zipped across like a superhero.”

Alex’s shoulders lifted, and the corners of his mouth tugged into almost a smile. That was true.

That evening, Alex slumped at the kitchen table. "I'm just bad at schoolwork," he muttered.

Grandpa, who was folding the newspaper, looked up. "Bad? No. Everybody has easy things and hard things. That's normal. Don't forget there are also things that you're good at."

Alex frowned. "Like what?"

The wooden chair creaked as Grandpa leaned back. "I'm sure you can tell me three things yourself."

Alex thought. "I can climb fast. I can whistle really loud. And... I can tell funny jokes."

Grandpa raised an eyebrow. "Let's hear a joke, then."

Alex's face lit up, and his eyes opened wide as he suddenly sat up straight. "Okay. Why did the teacher wear sunglasses in class?"

Grandpa tilted his head. "Why?"

"Because her students were so bright!" Alex laughed so hard he nearly tipped out of his chair.

Grandpa chuckled. "See? That's also part of who you are. School is important, but it's not all of you."

The next morning, Alex sat down with another tough math problem. His stomach felt tight again. But he remembered Grandpa's words.

He slid the blocks into neat rows, one by one, until the answer came. He wasn't as fast as the others. But it worked for him.

And later, when it was time for reading, he raised his hand to read. His voice shook, but he made it through one whole line.

Jamal and a couple of other classmates clapped softly. Alex felt a small smile spread across his face. He wasn't great at everything. But he was still Alex — and that was enough.

HERO LESSON

Some things are easy, others are hard.
You don't have to be good at everything,
just keep trying your best.

What about you?

- What is something that feels hard for you?
- What are some other things you know you're good at?

BADGE CHALLENGE

When something feels hard, and you feel like giving up, complete these two steps to earn the **Try Your Best** Hero Badge:

O Step 1: Write down (or say out loud) three things you're good at.

O Step 2: Take one small step to keep going on the hard thing.

This badge is yours when you finish the two steps and keep trying your best, even when it's tricky.

What did you do to earn this Hero Badge?

____

____

Ask a grown-up to approve below and start coloring!

You earned the Try Your Best badge!

Signed by: ____________________ Date: __________

DYLAN PLAYS CATCH

The kids gathered in the grassy lot after school, tossing baseballs back and forth as they warmed up. Leather gloves smacked as the balls landed in them.

Dylan jogged into place with the others, excited for the game to start.

Then Tyler came running up, grinning wide. “Look what I got for my birthday!” He held up a brand-new baseball. The white leather gleamed in the sunlight, the red stitches were sharp and perfect.

Tyler tossed the ball to Dylan for a closer look. Dylan turned it in his hands, tracing the stitches with his fingertips and squeezing the hard leather.

Dylan reached into his own glove and pulled out his ball. Its leather was soft and worn. The color had faded to yellow. It had green scuff marks, and the stitches were frayed from years of play.

He tossed his own ball into the air and caught it again. Compared to Tyler's, it felt dull and tired.

The game began. Gloves snapped, bats cracked, and kids shouted as they ran the bases. Tyler's new ball zipped fast and true, every throw bouncing clean into a waiting glove.

Dylan kept thinking about how bright and perfect it looked compared to his own ball.

At last, someone called, "Water break!" Tyler left his shiny ball beside his glove and walked across the grass to join the others near the sidewalk.

Dylan picked up Tyler's ball, his heart racing faster. As he started walking toward the others, he tossed the ball over his shoulder into a thick bush. The leaves rustled as the ball disappeared inside.

Heat rushed to his face even though nobody saw. He dropped onto the grass and forced himself to laugh with the others during the break.

When Tyler walked over to his spot again, he reached down and shouted, "Hey, where's my ball?"

"Check the grass!" one boy called. They crawled around, brushing through weeds. But the ball was nowhere to be found.

Dylan suggested, "Maybe a dog grabbed it while we were on break?" Dylan stared at the ground, hoping nobody would see he was lying.

Tyler's lip trembled. "It was my birthday present. My parents will be so mad." His glove dangled by his side as he shuffled home disappointed and sad.

The game broke up early. Dylan stayed silent, while his stomach twisted in a knot.

That evening, Dylan's mom answered the phone while he set the table. "Oh, hi Mrs. Ramirez... No, I didn't see an extra ball when I emptied the bags. But I'll ask Dylan."

She turned around. "Did you see Tyler's new ball?"

Dylan swallowed. "No. We couldn't find it."

Mom nodded slowly and returned to the call. "He says no. They can check the lot again tomorrow."

The next afternoon, the kids spread out in search of the lost ball. Tyler's face looked pale and worried. They searched for a long time.

Finally, Dylan moved closer to the bushes and shouted, "Hold on... I think I see something in that bush!"

He pointed quickly so everyone's eyes followed his finger. Then he ran over, reached in, and pulled the bright white ball from the leaves.

Tyler gasped. "You found it! You're the best, Dylan!" He clutched the ball tight. The others cheered.

Mom, watching from the sidewalk, raised her eyebrows. She said nothing, but then frowned.

That night, Dylan lay awake. Everyone believed he was a hero. But he still felt the knot in his stomach.

He wasn't caught at lying, but the bad feeling didn't go away so easily. He promised himself he wouldn't do it again.

HERO LESSON

Even if no one finds out,

a lie can still feel heavy inside.

What about you?

- Have you ever told a lie and kept pretending?
- How did that feel compared to telling the truth?

BADGE CHALLENGE

Talk with a grown-up and do these two honest steps to earn the **Truth Teller** Hero Badge:

O Step 1: Share a time you once lied and what it felt like to carry it.

O Step 2: If the person is still around, tell them the truth. If not, say out loud what you would say.

HERO BADGE

Coloring version

Find the full-color version in the welcome message!

You can earn this badge by talking to a grown-up and doing both of the honest steps.

What did you do to earn this Hero Badge?

____

____

Ask a grown-up to approve below and start coloring!

You earned the Truth Teller badge!

Signed by: ____________________ Date: __________

MASON'S MARBLE MACHINE

Mason's hair stuck out in three directions. His socks didn't match, but he rarely noticed. Mason was always a little distracted like that.

Sometimes the other kids teased Mason for how he looked, but he didn't really care. His mind was usually busy with other things.

In art class, Mr. Douglas said, "You may use any supplies today to build something."

Mason quickly filled his desk with toilet paper rolls, cardboard, and tape.

He connected toilet paper rolls, taped them to an empty cereal box, and set a paper cup at the bottom.

"A marble machine," he whispered.

He dropped a blue marble in at the top.
Clack. Roll.

It sped down the first tube. Then it hit a toilet roll cut in half, like a little halfpipe... **Swish!** The marble shot out over the edge and clattered to the floor.

He tried again. This time the marble shot into a tunnel, then... **Thunk!** The marble was stuck. Mason tipped the box and shook it, but nothing moved.

He dropped his shoulders and sighed. "It doesn't work," he muttered. He folded a paper airplane instead. It took five minutes, and it flew a short, crooked loop.

Mr. Douglas stopped by. "That's a fine plane," he said. Then he tapped the jumble of cardboard tubes. "But what's this?"

"My marble machine," Mason admitted. "I don't know how to fix it."

Mr. Douglas lifted one sagging tube. "See here? When it droops, the marble gets stuck. Builders add supports to keep things steady. Why don't you try again?"

Mr. Douglas set down his empty coffee cup with a clink. "Builders don't quit. They test, fix, and try again."

Mason blinked. "Okay."

He taped a popsicle stick under the bend. He pressed fresh tape along the tunnel seams. The marble made it further this time before it slipped off the side.

"Maybe make a fence," suggested Rory, leaning over from the next table. "Like a guardrail."

Mason folded a strip of paper, then taped it along the edge. He tried again.
Clack. Roll. Swoosh.

Almost — the marble hit the side of the paper cup, then bounced off.

By the end of class, Mr. Douglas circled back. Mason looked up nervously. "It's better... but it still misses the cup."

Mr. Douglas smiled and pointed to his empty coffee cup. "Think this would catch it? Builders also need the right piece at the right time."

Mason swapped the paper cup for the bigger china cup and taped it in place. He set the marble at the top.

Clack. Roll. Swoosh.

Ting!

The marble rang sharp and clear as it fell into the cup. Mason grinned. Rory clapped, and soon a few other classmates leaned closer to watch the marble go again and again.

Mr. Douglas nodded. "Excellent work. You finished what you started — and you weren't afraid to ask for help along the way. That's what real builders do."

Mason's socks still didn't match. His hair still stuck up. But this time, instead of feeling unsure, he felt proud.

He built it, fixed it, and finished it. Finishing what he started gave him confidence — and asking for help made it even better.

HERO LESSON

Finishing what you start builds confidence. And it's okay to ask for help when you're stuck.

What about you?

- Do you have something half-done — a sketch, a half-finished puzzle, or a half-built fort?

BADGE CHALLENGE

Only one simple step this time to earn the **Finisher** Hero Badge:

O Finish something you left half-done.

If you find it tricky, ask someone else for an idea or some help. Don't worry — that still counts for your badge!

HERO BADGE

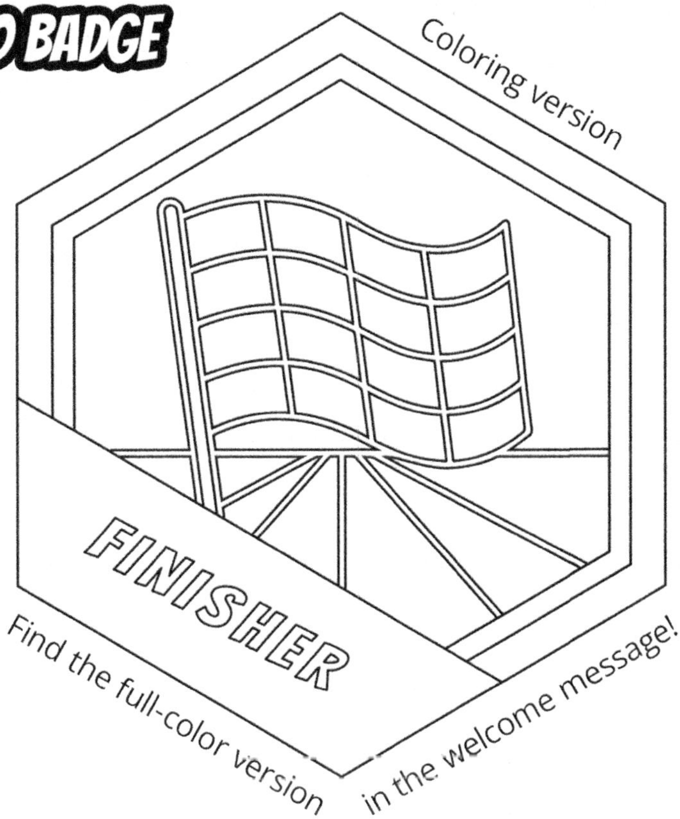

The badge is yours when you complete what you had left unfinished before.

What did you do to earn this Hero Badge?

____

____

Ask a grown-up to approve below and start coloring!

You earned the Finisher badge!

Signed by: ____________________ Date: __________

JULIAN AND DAISY

Julian dragged his backpack into Grandma's house. His parents had dropped him off for the week while they were away for work.

"Don't forget," Mom whispered before leaving, "take good care of Daisy."

Daisy was Julian's little brown puppy with floppy ears and an endless wiggle in her tail. She trotted behind him, her toenails click-clacking on the tiles.

Grandma patted Daisy's head. "She'll need feeding, walking, and lots of love. You're in charge this week, Agent Julian."

He grinned as he said, "Agent Julian promises to do

his duty!" He liked the sound of that.

At first, caring for Daisy felt like a game. Julian filled her bowl until the kibble piled high, then petted Daisy as she gobbled it down.

He showed off to Grandma by tossing three toys at once. He laughed when Daisy jumped between them, not sure which one to play with first.

But the next morning, Grandma frowned at the mess. "Julian, Daisy knocked her water everywhere. Did you refill it?"

Julian blinked. "Um... I thought she still had some."

Grandma shook her head gently. "Caring isn't about showing off. It's about showing up, even for the small jobs."

Julian's cheeks warmed. He promised himself he'd do better.

Two days later, Daisy whined at the back door. Julian was busy building a fort with cushions.

Out the window, he saw Grandma bent over her flower beds in the front yard.

"In a minute," he called to the puppy, stacking another pillow.

The whining continued for a while, but then it went quiet. Julian forgot all about Daisy.

Later, when he got bored with his fort, Julian peeked out the window. Grandma was now in her rocking chair on the porch, eyes closed in the warm sun.

Julian wandered through the house, looking for Daisy. When he reached the kitchen, he stopped cold.

A yellow puddle spread across the floor by the back door. Daisy sat a few feet away. Her ears drooped. Her eyes looked sad.

Julian's stomach sank. He wiped it up as fast as he could, hoping Grandma wouldn't see. His cheeks burned with guilt.

When he finally sat down on the cold kitchen floor, Daisy crept closer and licked his elbow.

He rubbed her soft ears. "You couldn't wait any longer," he whispered. "I left you waiting."

He now realized that Daisy needed him every day, not just when he felt like playing with her.

The next day, Agent Julian got Grandma's cooking timer out of the cabinet and put it on the counter. The tick-tick-tick made it sound like a secret gadget.

He used it to remind him to feed Daisy at breakfast, walk her after school, brush her before bed. Each ding reminded him to take care of Daisy.

By Friday, Daisy's tail wagged whenever Julian came near. She would jump up and try to lick his face.

It made him laugh and turn his face away from the smelly puppy breath. She then curled in his lap, happy and calm.

When Mom and Dad returned, Daisy leapt into their arms, healthy and joyful.

Mom hugged Julian tight. "You kept your promise."

He smiled, holding Daisy close. This time, Agent Julian had truly done his duty.

Caring wasn't about big shows or fun tricks. It was about being reliable, every day.

HERO LESSON

Caring for something or someone means showing up, not showing off.

What about you?

- Who or what do you help take care of at home?
- How can you make sure you show up every day, not just when it's fun?

BADGE CHALLENGE

Complete a one-week care schedule to earn the **Reliable Agent** Hero Badge:

O Step 1: Pick something small you can care for (a pet, plant, or daily chore).

O Step 2: Write or draw a planning schedule for your care task.

O Step 3: Follow your schedule every day for one week.

HERO BADGE

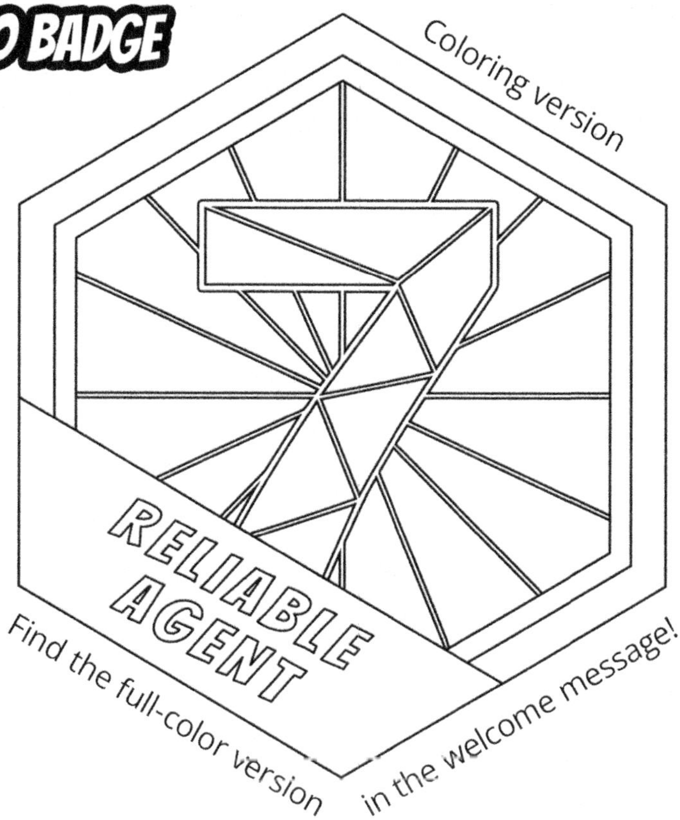

The badge is yours when you complete all seven days of care.

What did you do to earn this Hero Badge?

____

____

Ask a grown-up to approve below and start coloring!

You earned the Reliable Agent badge!

Signed by: ____________________ Date: __________

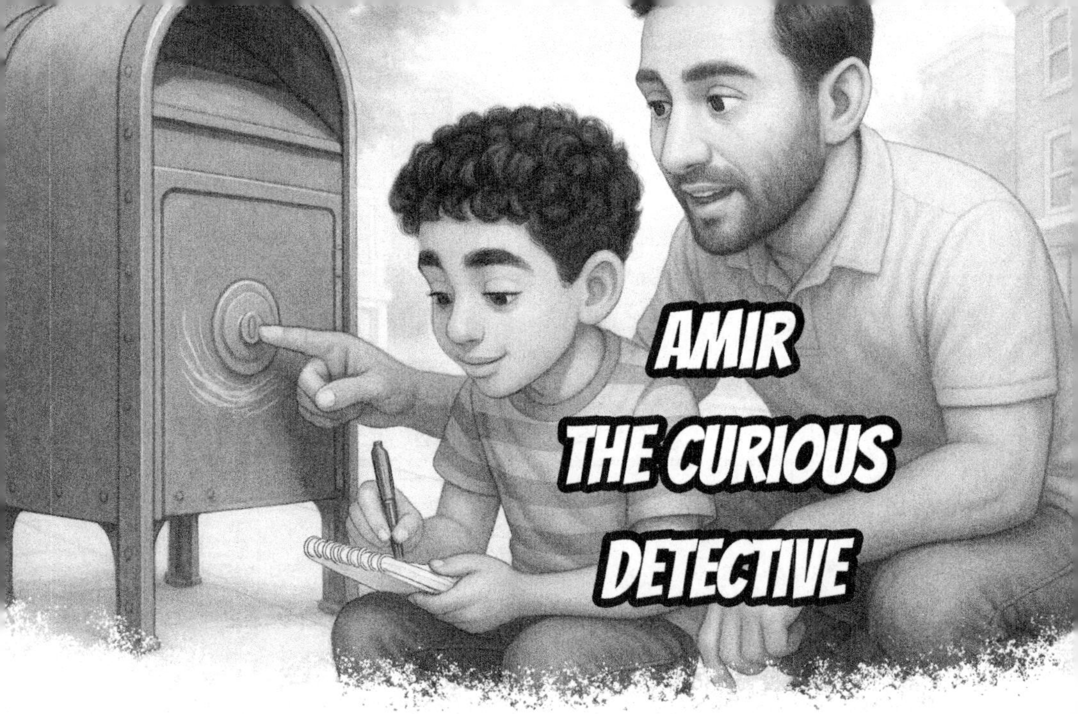

AMIR THE CURIOUS DETECTIVE

It was Saturday afternoon. Amir sat on the couch with his tablet propped against his knees and headphones clamped over his ears.

His fingers tapped the glowing screen only a few inches from his nose. He didn't even notice when Dad walked into the room.

A notebook dropped right in front of the tablet, blocking Amir's view. Startled, Amir pulled off his headphones and blinked up at Dad.

"I use this at work," Dad said. "But detectives need notebooks, too. Want to try?"

Amir sat up. The little flip notebook fit neatly in his

hand, with shiny rings at the top. It felt important.

He slid a pen through the spiral, just like he had seen Dad do so many times.

"Okay," Amir said. Then he asked, "But how can I be a detective?"

Dad smiled and said, "I'll be your partner. Come with me and I'll show you the first clue."

They stepped outside and walked over to the corner mailbox. "See the scratches around the lock?" Dad asked.

Amir looked closer. "Did someone try to break in?"

"At first I thought so, too," Dad said. "But the other day, I saw the mail carrier open it.

"Her big ring of keys scraped the paint as she turned the lock. That's what left the marks."

Amir tapped his pen against the page. "So the scratches tell a story!"

He wrote:
<u>Clue 1: mailbox scratches —> mailbox keys</u>

At the bus stop, Amir wrinkled his nose at white splatters on the pavement. “A painter left a big mess here,” he said.

“Don’t just look down,” Dad suggested.

Amir tilted his head back. A row of pigeons stared down at him from the power line above.

He laughed. “It’s not paint but bird poop! I’ll remember not to stand under here anymore.”

He scribbled:
Clue 2: mess below —> pigeons above

When almost home, Amir froze. A steady **Tap! Tap! Tap!** echoed from the apartment roof. He squinted, but couldn’t see what caused it.

“What’s making that sound?” he asked.

Dad shrugged. “Could be something loose. Or maybe an animal. Let’s just mark it down for now.”

Amir drew a question mark:
Clue 3: tapping sound —> rooftop?

Back at home, Amir flipped through his notebook.

"Two solved, one mystery."

Then he heard the mystery sound again, but only twice this time: **Tap! Tap!**

He rushed to the window, and saw a loose wire swinging in the breeze. He noticed that if the wind was strong enough, it struck the gutter each time.

Grinning, he changed his earlier note:
Clue 3: tapping sound —> ~~rooftop?~~ —> wire in wind

Dad nodded. "Detectives don't always find the answers right away. But they keep looking."

Amir asked, "Can everyone see clues like this?"

Dad said, "Yes, but not if they stare at screens or blast music in their ears. You have to pay attention to see that even ordinary places can be interesting."

Amir tucked the notebook into his pocket, proud to carry one just like Dad. The screen on the couch now seemed less exciting than his new notebook.

He already couldn't wait to go outside again and solve the next mystery.

HERO LESSON

Curiosity and observation can turn every day into an adventure.

What about you?

- Have you noticed any strange things?
- What did you discover when you looked more closely?

BADGE CHALLENGE

Next time you're going out, ask a grown-up to be your detective partner for a while.

Then try these steps to earn the **Clue Finder** Hero Badge:

O Step 1: Notice and write or draw 3 clues you might usually walk past.

O Step 2: Share your clues with your detective partner. Say what you think each one means, then ask what they think, too. That's what detective partners do.

HERO BADGE

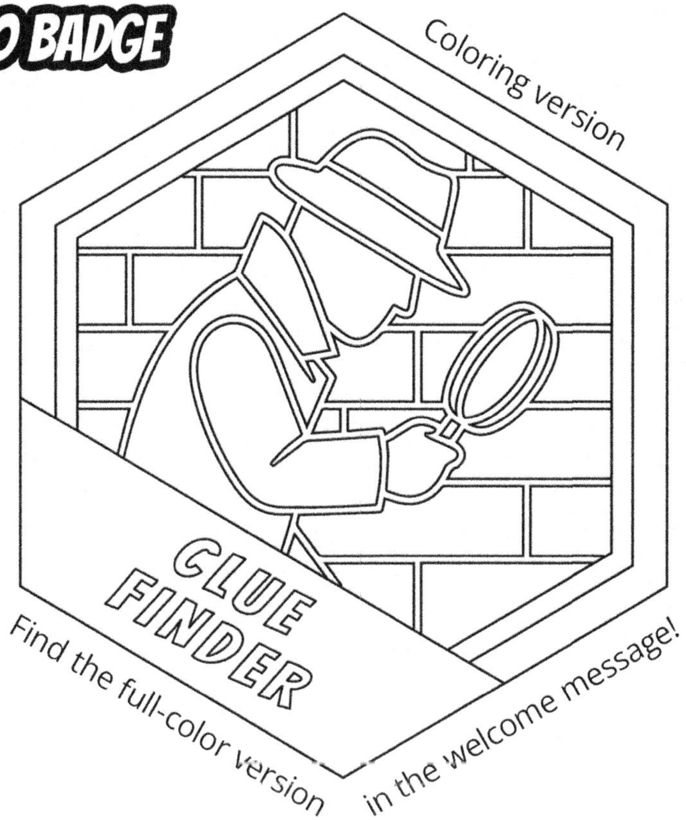

The badge is yours when you've completed your detective mission.

What did you do to earn this Hero Badge?

____

____

Ask a grown-up to approve below and start coloring!

You earned the Clue Finder badge!

Signed by: ____________________ Date: __________

AIDEN AND THE RAINBOW

Aiden pressed his forehead against the cool glass. Rain splashed against the window and ran in little rivers down the street.

A rumble of thunder sounded as he lay down onto the carpet. "Boring!" he complained. "No soccer today. No bike ride either."

Mom stood at the ironing board, steam puffing from the iron. "Storms can be useful, too," she said.

"They water the garden and fill the birdbaths for the robins. Sometimes even stormy days bring things to be thankful for."

Aiden rolled his eyes and tilted his head. "Thankful?

For this?" He pointed at the dark sky.

Just then another thunderclap cracked overhead. He jumped in a fright, then burst out laughing. "See, Mom? Even the sky disagrees with you!"

Mom shook her head with a smile, pressing the iron down across a sleeve. "You'll see."

Later, Dad came in dripping wet. "Practice was canceled," he said as he shook rain from his jacket.

While he took off his soaking shoes, he asked, "Now that I'm home early, want to keep working on our tower?"

"Sure!" Aiden said in surprise. So they continued to stack pieces until the tower wobbled as tall as his shoulders.

By evening, the rain had slowed to drips from the roof, and the clouds were breaking apart. When Aiden took out the trash, the air smelled fresh, like wet grass and earth.

But he froze when he looked up at the sky. "Mom! Dad! Come quick!" he shouted.

They came running and all three of them stood together in the yard to watch a rainbow stretch across the rooftops.

Aiden whispered, "Wow," as red, orange, yellow, and blue arched across the sky, with just a few clouds left. For a long moment, the three of them just stood still, looking up at the rainbow.

That night, Mom sat on Aiden's bed. "So... anything to be thankful for after all?"

Aiden rolled onto his back, thinking. "Dad came home early. We built the tower. And we saw that rainbow."

Mom nodded. "That's three. Think you can find three more tomorrow?"

The next day the sun shone, but puddles still dotted the driveway. Aiden stomped through one, water splashing up his legs and squishing in his sneakers. "Thanks, puddle," he laughed. "That was fun."

That night he listed his three things: "Pizza at lunch, a joke in class, and splashing puddles."

On the third day, he felt chilly on the walk to school, and the puddles had dried up.

In art class, Aiden colored a poster with warm reds and cool blues. "Looks great," a classmate said, which made Aiden feel proud.

During a quick soccer game after lunch, his foot hit the rolling ball just right and — **Thump!** — it shot straight into the back of the net. They were losing the game, but his teammates cheered anyway.

After gym class in the afternoon, he tugged on a pair of fresh socks. They felt warm and dry against his feet, and felt great compared to the chilly morning.

That evening he told Mom: "Colorful poster, scoring a goal, and fresh socks."

By the end of the week, Aiden realized it wasn't so hard to be thankful for things.

Some days were rainy, others were sunny, but every day had something good. And now he was starting to notice them even while they happened, not just at bedtime.

HERO LESSON

When you look for good things,
you can find them every day.

What about you?

- What three things are you thankful for today?

BADGE CHALLENGE

Do both steps to
earn the **Three Cheers** Hero Badge:

O Step 1: At bedtime, name three things that made your day better and share them with a grown-up.

O Step 2: Keep it up for three days in a row.

HERO BADGE

You can unlock this final badge by practicing thankfulness for three days in a row.

What did you do to earn this Hero Badge?

____

____

Ask a grown-up to approve below and start coloring!

You earned the Three Cheers badge!

Signed by: ____________________ Date: __________

Printed in Dunstable, United Kingdom

80569427R00047